RITA HAYWORTH
IN HER OWN WORDS

RITA HAYWORTH
IN HER OWN WORDS

Compiled by Neil Grant

HAMLYN

ART EDITOR: ROBIN WHITECROSS
RESEARCH BY MARGARET WOMERSLEY
PRODUCTION: ALISON MYER
PICTURE RESEARCH: EMILY HEDGES AND ANNA SMITH
EDITOR: SIAN FACER

THIS EDITION PUBLISHED IN 1992 BY PAUL HAMLYN PUBLISHING LIMITED,
PART OF REED INTERNATIONAL BOOKS LIMITED,
MICHELIN HOUSE, 81 FULHAM ROAD, LONDON SW3 6RB

A CATALOGUE RECORD FOR THIS BOOK IS AVAILABLE FROM THE BRITISH LIBRARY

ISBN 0 600 57459 8

PRODUCED BY MANDARIN OFFSET - PRINTED IN HONG KONG

CONTENTS

To Aunt Elina

he as wonderful a

damser as you are

is my hearts des

Dearest Love

Margarita

1931.

6

PAID TO DANCE

*"My parents were living in a theatrical hotel
in New York when I was born, which perhaps made me
a vaudeville veteran at birth"*

A lot of the Hollywood immortals sprang from nowhere in show-business terms, but there was never any doubt that Rita Hayworth would be a dancer. Her mother, Volga Haworth (no Y), had run away from a respectable home at sixteen to join the Ziegfield Follies. Her father, one Eduardo Cansino, was a Spanish dancer, a member of a dancing family that also claimed to trace its lineage back to the Middle Ages. At twenty-one, when he met Volga, he was already earning $1,500 a week, very big money in 1916.

Margarita Carmen Dolores Cansino, the future Rita Hayworth, was born on October 17, 1918. Eduardo was disappointed that she wasn't a boy, but two boys came along soon enough. Their mother gave up her career for family life, while Rita started dancing lessons with her uncle, Angel Cansino, who ran a dancing school in the neighborhood of Carnegie Hall, at the age of four. She joined the family vaudeville act, known predictably enough as The Dancing Cansinos, at eight.

The Cansino family finances, like those of many others', took a sharp blow in the slump of 1929. By that time, Rita's father had given up dancing in favor of choreography and teaching, but in 1931, business being slack, he decided to take up dancing again with a new partner – his daughter. At thirteen, Rita's figure was already well developed, and between shows in nightclubs in such racy places as Caliente and Tijuana, her father made sure she did not venture out of the dressing room. He had noticed the look in the eyes of male customers.

By the time she was fifteen, Rita had appeared as an extra in several films shot in Hollywood and Tijuana. She was often taken as Mexican, her natural coloring being dark. Several film people showed interest, and she did a screentest for Warner Brothers, but it came to nothing. Louella Parsons, queen of the Hollywood gossips, first met her soon

"Every girl who wants to dance should start training when she is young. I don't mean at four as I did, but while she is still ambitious and able to 'take it'"

afterwards, with Winfield Sheehan of Fox. The girl looked very Spanish and was painfully shy, her voice so low she could hardly be heard. Star material? Hardly, thought Louella.

In spite of such a negative assessment, Sheehan was impressed, and the Fox studio duly signed Rita (or rather, as she was under age, her father signed for her). She was sent to coaches in voice, acting and deportment — the normal grooming for potential starlets in the early days of the talkies. Dieting fiercely, she shed her puppy fat without losing her voluptuousness, and she took swimming, riding and tennis lessons in case she got a part requiring one of those abilities. She first appeared, in a dance sequence, in an epic called *Dante's Inferno* (1935). The film was described by one its stars, Spencer Tracy, as one of the worst films made anywhere at any time, but Rita, out from under her father's protective but oppressive thumb, was having some fun at last (though she still lived at home and her father controlled her social life, even chaperoning her on dates). In *Under the*

Pampas Moon she actually had a few lines – though on the set she forgot them, through nerves – and she had a few moments as a moderately devastating houri in *Charlie Chan in Egypt*, while in *Paddy O'Day* she had a leading role. There was talk of remaking *Ramona*, a big success of the silent era, in the new Technicolor with Rita as the lead. Rita set great store on *Ramona*, which looked like being the vehicle to make her a genuine star, and prepared diligently for the role. (Over thirty years later, she said she could still remember the lines.)

Then came disaster. Fox merged with Twentieth Century Productions, and Darryl F. Zanuck became the new studio boss. Sheehan was booted out, and Zanuck produced his own candidate for Ramona – Loretta Young. A few days after learning that she had lost the part, Rita, still only eighteen, was told the studio was not going to renew her contract. It looked as though a promising career had been nipped in the bud. Rita Cansino was just another starlet who hadn't made it. But Rita Hayworth just hadn't got started yet.

"I knew how to dance as soon as I was able to walk
and by the time I was four years old I had already appeared with
my father and my aunt in a Carnegie Hall recital"

"I used to study Spanish and tap dancing for four or five hours
a day and it was no cinch, especially having a father who was so
very strict. It was hard and tedious work and there were
times when I didn't think I could go on. But I did and, of course,
as it turned out the effort was worth it"

"I developed a burning ambition –
as only a too-fat seventeen-year-old can burn –
to become a good actress"

"It didn't require me to be a genius
to realize Fox was spending a great deal of time and money
on my behalf and I intended them to get their money's worth"

"I was also halfway responsible for earning the family's only
income at that time and we were a very close family.
The dancing school barely paid it's own operating costs.
I think my father's strictness was well justified
and certainly indicated his love and concern for my well-being"

"At home I'd lock myself in the bathroom,
stand in front of a mirror over the sink, and practise for hours.
I learned to correct flaws in my posture and pose for pictures in the
studio gallery for hours without complaining"

"I wanted to break into the movies, but I didn't know how.
I saw a director looking at me and heard him say to an assistant,
'It's too bad she doesn't speak English.'
I went up to him and said, 'Mister, I'm trying to learn Spanish.'
You should have seen the blank look on his face"

THE LADY IN QUESTION

"Perhaps if I hadn't been so shy and unsure of myself
I wouldn't have been so malleable"

Rita Hayworth's is the classic Hollywood story of the nice girl who is manufactured into a star, exploited by everyone in sight and finally destroyed by her own image. The sad case of Marilyn Monroe may be the more notorious, but there is a suspicion that Marilyn was likely to have found life difficult even if she hadn't become the world's Number One sex symbol.

Rita Hayworth, who was in her day also the favorite star of every male's private fantasies, started off with fewer hang-ups. She would perhaps have had a happier, if duller, life if she had married, for instance, a lawyer in Des Moines.

It is often said that the fault is not really the system, it's the individual. After all, they didn't have to be film stars, and if they couldn't stand the heat, they should have got out of the kitchen. Maybe – and though the proportion of top film stars who have managed to achieve both happiness and longevity is extremely small, it is true that Rita Hayworth wasn't very good at looking after herself. Marriages (she had five) for example, were a disaster area.

The sad thing is: Rita was always anxious to please. Though capable of ferocious rages, she was fundamentally a shy, well-meaning, and ordinary person who, as far as her career was concerned was a thorough professional. She wasn't a particularly brilliant actress technically – few top movie stars are (or need to be) – although, later in her career, as her films got worse, her performances got better (another familiar Hollywood syndrome). Nobody – until she began to crack up – ever had any criticism of her approach to her work. In fact, few serious people have anything bad to say about her at all. Besides lust and jealousy, she inspired a good deal of affection. 'Whatever you write about Rita,' Glenn Ford admonished a journalist, 'be gentle and kind – that's the kind of lady she was.'

"The screen affords a lot of discipline that people aren't aware of. Getting up at five o'clock on a cold morning for location shots in Utah isn't a luxury"

More often than not, a dominant male featured in Rita's life. After her father it was Ed Judson, who promised (justifiably) that he could further her career and, despite being older than her father, married her in 1937. He got her a number of small parts in independent movies, mostly low budget Westerns, in 1936-37 and finally persuaded Harry Cohn of Columbia to sign her up.

Cohn, certainly another of the dominant males in Rita's life, insisted on abandoning her Latin-sounding name, and she became Rita Hayworth. She began working very hard, turning out eight pictures in 1937. *Hit the Saddle Girls Can Play* (captain of girls' softball team, bumped off by poisoned baseball mitt), *Paid to Dance* the titles indicate the quality of these B pictures whose shooting schedule was seldom more than ten days.

She also went through the grooming process, which included altering her hairline by electrolysis, and the inevitable publicity-seeking nightclub round. She almost got a part in an A movie with Katherine Hepburn, then – a big break – was cast by Howard Hawks in *Only Angels Have Wings*. Judson also hired her an enterprising press agent who, after telling a lot of lies about the amount of money Rita spent on her wardrobe, got her on to the cover of *Look* magazine. Combined with her success in *Angels*, this marked her arrival as a star – especially as Columbia at that time had very few. MGM borrowed her for a role in a Joan Crawford picture, *Susan and God*, in which she dances a spectacular rumba, then she returned to Columbia to make *The Lady in Question* (1940) with Glenn Ford and director King Vidor.

The film, though a marked improvement on the B picture days, didn't set Hollywood on fire, but the team was one which was destined to make a very big impact a few years later. Soon afterwards she was cast in the lead as *The Strawberry Blonde* (after Anne Sheridan had walked out), the film which turned her more or less permanently into a redhead.

"I owe every thing to Ed.

I could never have made the grade in Hollywood without him.

I was just too backward. My whole career was his idea"

"I never had to do any fighting for myself

with executives and agents. He fought for me.

After we got married, running my career was his only concern

and he gave it everything he had, and his efforts paid off"

OF HER FIRST HUSBAND ED JUDSON

"All women like being being fussed over and I'm no exception.
I think it's damned nice!"

"I like having my picture taken and being a glamorous person.
Sometimes when I find myself getting impatient
I just remember the times I cried my eyes out because nobody
wanted to take my picture at the Trocadero
[A fashionable Hollywood nightclub]"

COVER GIRL

"A girl is a girl.
It's nice to be told you're successful at it"

Darryl Zanuck, who had dropped Rita without much ceremony, was forced to hire her back to play the femme fatale role, seducing bullfighter Tyrone Power, in *Blood and Sand*. It wasn't a good film, but it was a big film, and though Rita was still billed below the title, it shot her to the top of the Hollywood pole.

It was followed by her first film with Fred Astaire, *You'll Never Get Rich*. Rita was, after all, a dancer first, though the Columbia studio seemed unaware of it until then. The partnership, though short (Astaire was already past forty), was a terrific success: it's often forgotten that Rita, not Ginger Rogers, was Astaire's favorite partner.

A few weeks before the release of *You'll Never Get Rich*, the famous *Life* cover of Rita – kneeling on her bed in a satin nightdress – appeared. 'The Most Exciting Girl on the Screen!' blared Columbia publicity, and it was spot on. From this year (1941), Rita was the Number One Hollywood sex idol – a synonym for female glamor thoughout the world, her every word and action subject to the press speculation. The World War boosted her image even higher. Naturally, she had to live up to the part. She had separated from Judson, and had a succession of affairs with stars, of whom Victor Mature (her partner in *My Gal Sal*) looked, briefly, the most serious. In 1943 she married America's greatest cinema genius, Orson Welles. He couldn't resist her, and he was not an easy man to reject. Also, she fell in love with him. *Cover Girl* (1944) was supposed to feature 'Fifteen of the world's most beautiful girls' (New York models in fact), but it starred only the world's most beautiful woman. Taking a belated honeymoon with Welles in New York, Rita experienced the terror of being mobbed by obsessed fans.

Cohn disliked her marriage and, even more, he disliked its result. Rita became pregnant in 1944, and her daughter Rebecca was born in December. A few weeks later Rita's mother died, still only forty-five. These two events, which affected her marriage, also gave Rita some temporary doubts about her career. They were not shared by Cohn, who had limited her

"I love the notion of those little volcanoes going off inside that he says he senses in me on the screen"

OF KENNETH TYNAN, PROMINENT LONDON CRITIC

films to one a year, and work went ahead on *Gilda*, in which she was reunited with Glenn Ford – back from naval service – and once again directed by King Vidor.

Gilda marks her apotheosis as sex queen. It's a strange movie, characteristic of the time, psychologically complex, deriving extra punch from the real-life involvement of its two stars, and today enjoying cult status. It contained a song-and-dance number (Rita was dubbed, to her annoyance) in which she wears the slinky, strapless, black dress that became forever associated with her — a scene of such powerful eroticism, with Rita swinging her magnificent hair about to such effect that one clergyman even wrote to threaten her hairdresser with the fires of hell!

However, the problem experienced by all actors famous for a particular role: is that the public expects them to be like that character. This didn't matter much if you were, say, Mae West. But if you were Rita Hayworth, it could be a trial. For Rita was nothing like Gilda.

Her next picture for Columbia was a fan-tasy-musical, *Down to Earth*, which did well because any film starring Rita Hayworth would have done well at that time. The publicity people were having fun. Rita's face appeared on the first atom bomb tested after the end of the war (she was not consulted about that tasteless stunt).

Following a short-lived reconciliation, she went on to make a rather different sort of picture with Welles, *The Lady from Shanghai*, in which her hair was cut short and dyed blonde. The public didn't like it, didn't like the film either (Rita's character dies on screen), though it's now acknowledged as one of Welles's best.

Rita was sent to Europe in 1947 on a publicity jaunt, attending the London premiere of *Down to Earth*. She was now approaching thirty, and she still looked magnificent. She enjoyed the trip so much she went again, against Cohn's wishes, after making *The Loves of Carmen* — back to Spanish dancing again — with a hopelessly miscast Glenn Ford in 1948. On this trip she met Aly Khan, and the result of that meeting was that she made no films for four years.

"*Dancing is my natural heritage, and I have always loved it.*
But I always hated to practise.
But rehearsals with Fred Astaire were occasions I found myself
looking forward to with an anticipation of pleasure"

"*I guess the jewels of my life were the pictures I made with Fred*
*Astaire. When he came to do two films at Columbia, he **asked** for*
*me. Fred **knew** I was a dancer. He knew what all those dum-dums*
at Columbia didn't know, and if it hadn't been for him I would
never have been cast in either film"

*"I wanted privacy,
but that seems impossible with
the American press"*

*"It was Harry Cohn's idea to
put my picture on that bomb.
I was under contract, and they
threatened to put me on
suspension if I put up a fuss.
Harry was... the Gestapo
at Columbia. I hate war. That
whole bomb thing made me sick
to my stomach"*

"Two things"

ASKED WHAT KEPT UP HER DRESS IN THE GILDA
SONG-AND-DANCE NUMBER

*"[Men] fell in love with 'Gilda',
but they woke up with me"*

*"I never really thought of
myself as a sex goddess.
I felt I was more a comedian
who could dance"*

*"I don't suppose anyone who knows me gives me much credit
for being a brainy dame"*

*"I'm a good actress. I have depth. I have feeling.
But they don't care.
All they want is the image"*

*"I like them all — for different reasons of course.
In Spain, where my father came from, and in Mexico, where I have
lived, a girl's worth is judged by the number of suitors she has!
I'm not out to corner the bachelor market in Hollywood but I do
enjoy window-shopping whenever I can"*

OF HOWARD HUGHES, DAVID NIVEN, TONY MARTIN, AND ORSON WELLES

"I'm no Einstein – but I'm willing to learn.
Orson's the most stimulating man I've ever known..."

"You see, Orson was trying something new with me,
but Harry Cohn wanted The Image –
The Image he was going to make me
till I was ninety!"

ON HER CHANGE OF STYLE FOR *THE LADY FROM SHANGHAI*

*"You know, the only
happiness I've ever had in my
life has been with you"*
TO ORSON WELLES

*"I knew it was a classic
while we were making it"*
OF LADY FROM SHANGHAI

*"He was tormented,
possessive, insecure..., a genius,
crazy like a horse,
and a marvellous man,
completely unaware of reality"*
OF ORSON WELLES

37

THE LOVES OF CARMEN

"I didn't want five husbands,
but it happened that way and that's all there is to it"

Rita Hayworth certainly fulfilled all expectations of a Hollywood glamor queen, no less in her not-so-private life than through her public image. Her name was linked at various times with a great many men, including some of the most attractive male stars of her day. Whether she had physical affairs with all, or even most, of them seems doubtful. Since practically every heterosexual male wanted to possess her, at least temporarily, and the ones she happened to know tended to be at once the most desirable and the most egotistical, the chances of her making a solid and suitable marriage were slight to say the least. As she said herself, men tended to fall in love with Gilda, but woke up with her.

She married five times; none of her marriages lasted more than a few years.

Her first husband was the slightly mysterious operator Ed Judson, a kind of Svengali figure, far too old, who was chiefly interested in her earning potential. Her second was Orson Welles, a Beauty and Brains alliance like that of Monroe and Arthur Miller later and equally doomed. In fact, Orson seems to have been about as loving a husband as Rita ever had, but he was hardly the kind of man to stay at home in the evenings and help cook the dinner. This failure in the domestic sphere of their life was given as the main reason for the breakdown of their marriage, which makes it all the more odd that Rita's next husband should have been the playboy prince, Aly Khan.

Rita fell for Aly's charm, of which he had plenty. Unfortunately, he had little else to recommend him, at any rate as a husband, and whether or not it is true that he was sleeping with other girls in the very week of their wedding, they had nothing in common and Rita did not like the kind of society in which he moved – the European jet set as it would be called now.

It was during her courtship, marriage and divorce of Aly that Rita suffered most from the attentions of the popular press, and that alone was surely enough to break up a marriage.

> ## *"At least six, I would imagine,*
> ## *but it's really difficult for me to say since seventeen has always*
> ## *been my lucky number"*
>
> ON HOW MANY HUSBANDS A CAREER WOMAN SHOULD HAVE

The couple were ceaselessly front-page news, and insolent reporters would stop at almost nothing to break into their privacy. Rita grew accustomed to escaping from hotels through basement windows and up ladders to a backstreet. She had only to shut her eyes for a moment, and the media reported that she was exhausted, or fed up, or pregnant, or drunk (she did drink too much sometimes: it was one subject of complaint from Aly who, as a Muslim, was a teetotaller). She had a daughter, Yasmin, by Aly, who accepted Rebecca, her daughter by Welles. But she deluded herself if she really supposed that Aly would adapt himself to the sort of family life she would undoubtedly have liked. There were all kinds of other negatives. Rita was a Catholic, but the marriage (a civil ceremony performed by the mayor of Cannes who was, incidentally, a Communist) wasn't recognized by the Vatican, and even money problems – Aly was a big spender but with no actual resources of his own, and the breakdown of

the marriage left Rita, for a time, short of cash, absurd though that may seem. (Harry Cohn used this to sign a new contract on terms less advantageous to Rita.)

Rita's marriage to Aly broke up early in 1951 – though there were some later attempts at reconciliation, and the winding up of the marriage became an epic saga on its own. Her divorce came through in January 1953, and later that year she married a sub-Sinatra crooner called Dick Haymes, partly perhaps to spite Harry Cohn. Haymes, whose nickname was 'Mister Evil', was the least satisfactory of all her husbands. Rita's friends, justly or not, held him partly responsible for her accelerating decline. By the time she married the producer James Hill, in 1958, alcohol had become a problem, and though she enjoyed a brief period of reasonably tranquil domesticity, tales of sudden furious rows circulated. Hill himself later recorded a dreadful scene which culminated in a gun being fired. In September 1961 Rita filed for divorce.

"I married for love,

but he married me for an investment"

"My husband was always finding fault with me.

He was extremely jealous and quarrelsome"

"I never had any fun.

I was never permitted to make any decisions.

From the first he told me

I couldn't do anything for myself.

My personality crawled deeper and deeper into a shell"

OF ED JUDSON

"Maybe I tried hardest to be a good wife
in my second marriage.
I really wanted to be everything Orson wanted of me"

"I couldn't take his genius any more...
I was married, yet I didn't have a husband...
He told me he never should have married in the first place,
as it interfered with his freedom in his way of life"

OF ORSON WELLES

"I saw him in Spain a few years ago.
He had gotten so fat!
And he was such a handsome man when I married him.
He's a genius, there's no doubt about that.
But I don't think living with a genius is any more difficult
than living with me!"

"Orson never had any respect or regard for money,
that's always been his biggest problem.
And, believe it or not, I do worry a lot about him"

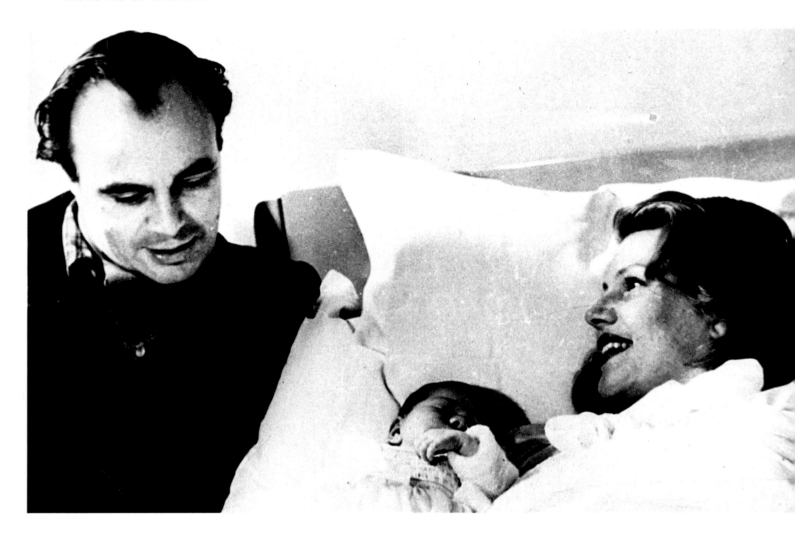

"I had no idea who he was.

He had something, to do with a famous family, that's all I knew.

I think this rather amused him"

"I am lost in a kind of dream world"

"I loved him.

He had such an overwhelming effervescence

that he sort of devoured you.

The world was magic when you were with him"

OF ALY KHAN

"I couldn't stand his playboy habits"

"He doesn't understand family life.
He thinks only of gambling, horse-racing,
and big-game hunting"

"The main thing that I'm worried about
is Yasmin [daughter by Aly Khan].
I don't want any of his money in order to provide
for her upkeep. I'll renounce all such claims
just so long as I can keep her"

During divorce proceedings

"Contrary to popular belief that I'm a wealthy woman,
I don't have any money at all.
As a woman in love with her husband I can tell you
that you have no idea how horrible it is for me
to see Dick spending sleepless nights over his bills, penalties,
and income tax problems without being able to do anything
about it. I feel so helpless"

OF DICK HAYMES

"Listen, all my life I've had trouble
making up my mind about everything.
But one thing's easy. Whenever I'm threatened,
I do just the opposite"

"I could hardly believe I could be a princess one minute
*and be treated like **that** the next"*

"I stood by him as long as he was in trouble,
but I can't take it any more"
ON DICK HAYMES

"Am I happy in this marriage? I sure am!"
ON JAMES HILL

*"He would come in the door, go straight to his room
and wouldn't even talk to me all night.
He said I was not a nice woman in too loud a voice"*

*"I don't remember what year it was —
I do remember it was Ground Hog Day"*

ASKED BY A DIVORCE LAWYER FOR THE DATE OF HER MARRIAGE TO HILL

"I feel I have so much to live for in my two little girls.
I'm going to keep working hard to take care of them and give them
the advantages they should have"

"My girls and I are everything to each other.
Sometimes I would refuse work to make it possible
for us to be together"

"There's always been some man in my life.
But marriage? Me? Again?
Well, I'd have to think about that a long time"

ONLY ANGELS HAVE WINGS

"If I had a word of advice for newcomers it would be,
'Don't plan anything'"

After leaving Aly Khan, Rita went back to work at Columbia. Her first film was *Affair in Trinidad* (1952), a patched-up romantic drama with a vintage Rita dance number, which cost a little over $1 million to make and took $7 million in receipts. The studio's publicity department had been at full stretch – and Rita hadn't lost her drawing power. *Salomé* followed, with Rita doing the Dance of the Seven Veils in order to save John the Baptist rather than condemn him – a ridiculous film, Rita thought, rightly. The best performance was by a camel, which had previously carried Marlene Dietrich.

She was still the Love Goddess, but becoming more of a Juno than a Venus. She didn't, apparently, resent the inevitable progression, since it gave her the chance to be an actress rather than a glamor girl. As Miss Sadie Thompson, she turned in a fine performance, but the film flopped. Rita was now drinking heavily, and caught up in the troubles of Dick Haymes with the Revenue Service and with the immigration authorities. Having always been a true pro, Rita was becoming difficult to deal with. Although *Fire Down Below* (1957), made in Trinidad with her two amiable co-stars, Jack Lemmon and Robert Mitchum, was a happy experience, and she went on to make *Pal Joey* with Cohn's new Love Goddess, Kim Novak. In the screen version of Terence Rattigan's play, *Separate Tables* (1958), she gave one of her best performances.

She was now a free agent, and Harry Cohn was dead. The dreadful Haymes episode faded at last, though her image had been permanently tarnished by it.

She got rave reviews for her next film *The Story on Page One*, this time in a thoroughly unglamorous role. There was talk of a stage appearance with Gary Merill, her latest lover, in 1962, but it did not come off. The truth was that Rita could not do it. During rehearsals, she was hospitalized for 'nervous exhaustion'. Her

"I haven't had everything from life.
I've had too much"

moods, forgetfulness, temperamental outbursts, were generally put down to drink. Though she was not yet fifty, the onset of Alzheimer's disease was probably partly responsible. TV projects, despite a few successful appearances, also tended to fizzle out, but she could still make films. As one critic said, she was making fewer, and less popular, movies, but giving better and better performances.

Her reviews for *The Money Trap* (1966) were the best yet. In another respect too, Rita functioned pretty well: she remained close to her daughters, now grown up. Robert Mitchum was responsible for getting her what turned out to be her last part in a movie, *The Wrath of God* (1972). The film was daft; Rita was OK. She signed up to make one more picture, a British horror job. The first day she walked on to the set, the cast and crew burst into applause, but

she couldn't get through it and fled the country — incurring a £1 million breach of contract lawsuit from World Films. Producers were now wary of her, and inability to get work made her increasingly depressed. She became almost a recluse. She made a few public appearances, but too often they ended in embarrassment. She had a facelift. She lapsed into spells of near-blankness. She became slightly paranoid.

There were one or two more public appearances – occasions to honor her with various awards – and she still looked good. Her daughter Yasmin began to see more of her. Old friends gathered round. But her career was over and the Love Goddess was leaving the set for good. At a court hearing in 1981 to appoint someone to look after her affairs, it was announced that she was suffering from Alzheimer's and required constant care.

"I don't **have** to make a picture. I don't have to work.

I don't have to make a name.

As for keeping my name in front of the public,

I don't have much trouble" 1949

"I'm choosing my own parts now.

I want to do pictures that are good,

and I want to play women that aren't just

beautiful and glamorous" 1958

"I looked at all the parts I had done and realized that, no matter how they were sliced, it was still Salomé"

"Everybody does nude scenes, but I don't. I never made nude movies. I didn't have to do that. I danced. I was provocative, I guess, in some things. But I was not completely exposed"

IN THE SIXTIES

*"This was the first chance I had to show Harry Cohn I could be
more than just a sex symbol.
I considered myself an actress too, and I'd be damned if I'd let him
screw me out of the opportunities of proving it"*
OF *MISS SADIE THOMPSON*

*"There is nothing more ageing to a woman's appearance than the
awful strain of trying to look young"*

*"That's one problem I don't have, Honey.
I never get up until the afternoon"*
ASKED BY A REPORTER HOW SHE FELT WHEN SHE LOOKED IN THE MIRROR EVERY
MORNING AND REALIZED SHE WAS NO LONGER THE LOVE GODDESS

"Apart from anemia and fatigue,
there is nothing wrong with my health or my outlook.
It is ridiculous for anyone to say
I am at the end of my rope" 1962

"But I'm not as old as [Bette] Davis or [Joan] Crawford.
I want to work. Can you get me any work?
You already have a lot of old stars?
*Honey, I'm not an **old** star, I'm an actress"*

CONVERSATION WITH AN AGENT, RECORDED BY JOHN KOBAL, 1973

"I have no regrets.
Life has taught me that if you want something
badly enough you'll go after it, no matter what the odds are.
In the long run,
I think this is the right thing to do"

"I never felt like one of those movie queens they used
to manufacture in Hollywood. I had sexy genes, I guess,
and that helped"

"I don't look back. I did what I had to do.
I was the property of Columbia..."

PICTURE CREDITS